The Common-wealth v. You

A PRACTICAL GUIDE *to the* **PENNSYLVANIA CRIMINAL JUSTICE SYSTEM** *for* **INDIVIDUALS** *facing* **CHARGES**

R. Davis Younts, ESQ

Client Testimonials

Very professional, knowledgeable, full of integrity and reputable man, whose skills and passion make his clients and law work together at their best.

– Alena

I always wondered how an attorney could represent a "criminal." After working with this attorney, I completely understand. He is so intelligent and caring. He achieves the best results for his clients as possible. I have been so impressed and amazed by the depth of knowledge. He embraces federal, state, and military clients and does not judge, but challenges and achieves fair results. I had the gracious opportunity to work alongside him in the final stages of Corey Walker's release from prison. Corey came and had a sit down with us in the days following his release along with his sister. I will never forget the conversations that day.

– Christine

I want to thank you for helping me out in my federal case. You spoke to me with compassion and understanding. You advised me every step of the way. You answered all my questions and concerns. I cannot express to you the gratitude that my family and I have for the hard work and fight that you did for me. Keep up the wonderful work.

– Edmee

Through the hardest time of my life Davis showed compassion and care when handling my case. I could not recommend a better person/lawyer to help through a difficult situation. Thank you, Davis, for everything.

– Katelyn

There aren't enough words to describe how Mr. Younts has helped my family and me and continues to do so to this day. He is highly intelligent, respectful, very knowledgeable, courageous; I can go on and on. If you need a lawyer or need help finding a good lawyer, he is your go to. I am happy to have met and him. Vote for Younts!!!

– Jade

I hired Mr. Younts firm to represent me in a serious, difficult matter, and I was extremely pleased with the hard work, dedication, and effort displayed. Mr. Younts gave excellent personal service, answered all of my concerns, and did an excellent job during my hearing making a reasoned argument and guiding me personally during a difficult and unfamiliar process. I would most definitely hire him again and encourage others to hire him for his expertise and excellent work.

– Jim

Contents

Chapter 1

Facing Criminal Charges?

I remember the feeling vividly ... sitting in a courtroom prosecuting my first case. I had gone to law school and was a licensed attorney. I had received specialized training in trial advocacy from the Air Force, but was I really prepared?

Slowly, case after case, and jury trial after jury trial, I began to learn the system, learn the process, and began to understand effective courtroom advocacy. I also learned from observing the advocacy of other attorneys. While I am glad I had the opportunity to serve as a prosecutor, I found my true calling and passion when I had the opportunity to become an Air Force defense attorney. While I would go on to become a Senior Defense Counsel and serve as the Chief of the Military Justice division at the Air Force Judge Advocate General's School, it was my experience as a young defense attorney that really helped me understand the challenges an individual faces when they are accused of a crime.

The criminal justice system in Pennsylvania has developed slowly over time. In representing clients throughout the Commonwealth, I have learned that one of the most interesting aspects of the system is how the handling of cases and the processes used vary significantly from county to county. This variation is a reflection of the unique geographic and demographic variables of Pennsylvania's counties. Another interesting aspect of the system is that Judges and District Attorneys are elected officials. The system of popularly elected officials is intended to be a powerful tool for accountability, at times it is. Unfortunately, the system is not perfect, has flaws, and does not always get it right.

After almost two decades of serving clients during investigations and criminal trials, I am still learning. I understand from my own experience as a prosecutor, and defense attorney, how intimidating it can be for those who are facing charges to prepare for the case, fight to protect their innocence, and learn what they need to know so they can protect their future and freedom.

Anyone who is charged with a crime understands that it is truly the Commonwealth of Pennsylvania versus them. In fact, that is even how cases are titled; literally it is the

Commonwealth v. [*Insert Your Name Here*]. Even the name given to a case carries with it the intimidating reality that anyone who is suspected of a crime has transitioned from an average citizen, co-worker, and neighbor to a defendant facing down the full power and authority of the government of Pennsylvania.

It is my hope that this book will serve as a guide for you and your family if you are facing the overwhelming prospect of criminal prosecution. This is a guide designed to help you understand the process and begin to prepare your defense. It is not meant to be a substitute for legal advice, and you should be discussing everything covered in this book with your attorney.

The Pennsylvania Rules of Criminal Procedure (Pa.R.Crim.P.) create the statewide framework for criminal prosecutions. Counties may also create and publish local criminal court rules that are specific to that county and are used in conjunction with the Pa.R.Crim.P. The purpose of these rules is to ensure that the rights of defendants are protected, cases are handled with a measure of consistency throughout the state, and that cases are handled in a timely, well-ordered process.

Despite the tremendous stress and the challenges that come with defending yourself against criminal charges in Pennsylvania, it is important to know that with the proper preparation, representation, and focus—you can receive a fair trial and win the fight to protect your future and your freedom.

In the almost two decades I have spent in Pennsylvania and military courtrooms all over the world and in teaching and training defense attorneys and military JAGs, I remain convinced that citizens of Pennsylvania can, and most often due receive fair trials and that Pennsylvania juries are typically composed of citizens who are primarily motivated by the desire to follow the law and do the right thing.

The challenge individual defendants face is ensuring their rights are protected in the midst of a government-run system that is often feels overrun and overburdened with cases. Although there are constitutional protections and many fair-minded judges, it only takes one visit to a county courthouse in Pennsylvania to realize how easy it is for an individual and their case to get lost in the system. From overworked defense attorneys who have never met their client before the day of a hearing, to impatient courthouse personnel who have to raise their voices and bark commands out in an effort to simply keep order, it often seems as if an individual is just a number that is being rushed through a process with little consideration of the uniqueness of their situation or the fact that their future and freedom is at stake. After observing this over and over again, it has become my hope and passion that defendants will always be represented by an attorney who understands not only the law but also how difficult going through the process of criminal prosecution is for individuals and their families. Regardless of who represents them, defendants must take ownership of their own case and future by learning as much as they can about the process and doing everything they can to prepare for their trial. It is my hope and desire that this book will help.

Chapter 2

Know Your Rights

American citizens and citizens of Pennsylvania have basic Constitutional rights. Understanding how these rights play a role in criminal prosecutions is critical to ensuring the rights have practical value. The most important rights to understand when under investigation and facing criminal charges are the right to remain silent and the right to be represented by an attorney.[1]

You Have the Right to Remain Silent!

You have the right to remain silent and the right to consult with an attorney before answering the questions of a police officer. Understanding these rights, and how to

---

[1] These rights are grounded in the Fourth, Fifth, and Sixth Amendments of the United States Constitution.

ensure that you do not waive them can be critical to the outcome of your case.

TV and movies have made being read your rights if you are arrested a recognizable, shared cultural experience. Most people can quote almost verbatim their right to remain silent and consult an attorney. What many people do not realize, until it is too late, is that you may be interrogated or questioned by police in a "non-custodial" setting without being read your rights. What the law requires is that you are read your rights before being questioned after you are taken into custody and no longer free to leave.[2] However, whether you are in custody or not, no one can force you to make an incriminating statement or consent to any search or seizure of your property.

As recognized by the United States Supreme Court, a suspect or defendant in a criminal case in Pennsylvania has a number of fundamental legal rights among them is the right to remain silent. If the police attempt to question you in connection with an alleged crime, you do not have to answer their questions, and it is strongly in your best interest to consult with an attorney before saying anything.

---

[2] *Miranda v. Arizona*, 384 U.S. 436 (1966), was a landmark decision of the U.S. Supreme Court in which the Court ruled that the Fifth Amendment to the U.S. Constitution prevents prosecutors from using a person's statements made in response to interrogation while in police custody as evidence at their trial unless they can show that the person was informed of the right to consult with an attorney before and during questioning, and of the right against self-incrimination before police questioning. In addition, the police must demonstrate that the defendant not only understood these rights, but voluntarily waived them.

This right to remain silent exists under the Fifth Amendment to the U.S. Constitution, and it applies in state criminal cases under the Equal Protection Clause of the Fourteenth Amendment. The relevant language in the Fifth Amendment states: "No person shall be . . . compelled in any criminal case to be a witness against himself . . ." Practically what this means is that if you are being accused of a crime, you do not have to answer any questions, you do not have to provide access to your phone, and you do not have to voluntarily give the police any other evidence or information that could be used against you.

Far too many individuals who are under investigation believe that they should talk to the police and cooperate with law enforcement. They know they are innocent and believe they should explain themselves. This is almost always a critical mistake. Far too often, innocent individuals are manipulated into making statements that do significant damage to their case. From accusations of making a false statement to obstruction of justice, I have seen far too many defendants who were innocent of the original charges against them, go to jail because of statements they made to law enforcement that were later used against them. The FBI's actions in the case involving Retired General Mike Flynn provide a clear example of someone who was not found to have engaged in any criminal actions except lying to investigators. General Flynn was a visible member of the Trump administration, and his prosecution made headlines when the FBI Agent's notes were provided to his defense team. What those notes revealed was that if the FBI agents could not get General Flynn to admit to crime, their goal was to get him to lie so that they could prosecute him or get him fired. Unfortunately, that case demonstrates what many attorneys fear—that a otherwise innocent suspect may be prosecuted for something they say during the course of an investigation that is later used against them.

If you are asked to "come to the station" or speak with law enforcement, you should speak with an attorney before you answer any questions. It does not matter if you are innocent and simply trying to defend yourself. If you are being read your rights, it is because they believe you committed a crime; they are not looking to help you or just clear some things up. They are questioning you because they believe you are guilty.

If you are being questioned by law enforcement, it is also critical to remember that you should never let your guard down or be thrown off by the fact that you have not been read your rights. While your statements *might* end up being found inadmissible later by a judge, they may not be. The prosecution will do everything they can to use the statements, and in order to have inadmissible self-incriminating statements kept out of court, the burden will be on you to convince a judge that the police violated your constitutional rights . . . that is not a fight that defendants always win. Because of the complicated legal issues involved and the potential debate of what is considered being in police "custody," it is critical to consult with an attorney before answering questions, even if you have not been read your rights.

I have personally watched the videos and read the transcripts of dozens and dozens of interrogations where police either avoid reading defendants their rights by conducting "non-custodial" interrogations by convincing suspects to come to the station voluntarily. In other cases, the officer will find a way to convince suspects to waive their rights.

Police officers and other law enforcement personnel may attempt to manipulate you into waiving your rights even as they inform you of them. They will say, "this is just a formality" or "if you remain silent, then no one gets to hear your side of the story, and it will look bad." My favorite is this statement, "Look, I would love to help you out and tell the District Attorney that you were straight with me, but I can only do that if you talk to me." All of these tactics are designed to keep a suspect talking and making statements.

It is my hope that by understanding the right to remain silent is a basic constitutional right for a reason, and that criminal interrogations are inherently coercive defendants will understand and invoke their rights.

You Have the Right to be Represented by an Attorney!

In addition to the right to remain silent, all suspects have the right to be represented by an attorney.[3] Although it is important to remain silent, it is also important to exercise your right to legal counsel. You should clearly and vocally request to speak with an attorney. An attorney will then be able to deal with the police and prosecutors on your behalf, and you will be able to tell your attorney everything without fear of your statements being used against you.

Every county or local jurisdiction within Pennsylvania has a system to provide defendants who cannot afford an attorney, with representation.[4] The determination of whether a defendant qualifies for a public defender or court-appointed counsel is made by the court where the case is being heard. A defendant will be provided counsel if a determination is made that they do not have the ability to

---

[3] The Sixth Amendment provides that, "[i]n all criminal prosecutions, the accused shall enjoy the right to a speedy and public trial, by an impartial jury of the state and district wherein the crime shall have been committed, which district shall have been previously ascertained by law, and to be informed of the nature and cause of the accusation; to be confronted with the witnesses against him; to have compulsory process for obtaining witnesses in his favor, and to have the assistance of counsel for his defense."

[4] The right to be represented by court-appointed counsel is tied to whether or not a defendant faces the possibility of imprisonment. *See* Pa.R.Crim.P. Rule 122, *Argersinger v. Hamlin*, 407 U. S. 25 (1972), and *Coleman v. Alabama*, 399 U. S. 1 (1970).

retain their own lawyer. The seriousness of the charges, and the availability of resources to hire a lawyer, will determine whether a defendant qualifies for a public defender. For example, an individual charged with murder may be eligible for a public defender because of the high cost of hiring a private attorney. The same individual may not be eligible for a public defender if charged with writing a bad check.[5]

Typically, so-called "court-appointed" attorneys are either county employees that work in the public defender's office or what is called "conflict counsel" meaning they are paid by the county to represent clients when there is not a public defender available or the public defender's office is representing a co-defendant.

A challenge that I can relate to, from serving for several years as an appointed defense attorney in the military, is that appointed counsel are often limited in their ability to provide meaningful representation during the investigative stage of a case or feel pressure to assist as many clients as possible. Public defenders and appointed counsel are typically forced to engage in legal triage, where they have to decide which clients are the priority and try to make the best use of their limited time and resources. Because cases

---

[5] Some counties use the Federal Poverty Guidelines as a guide for determining eligibility. The 2020 Poverty Guidelines are determined based on the number of people in a household. For households with one person the poverty threshold is $12,760, the amount is raised by $4,480 for each additional household member. In counties using the federal poverty level as a guide, individuals making less than the poverty level will be presumed to be eligible for free counsel.

going to trial in the next days or weeks are the priority, and due to their caseload, appointed counsel are often unable to assist until after an investigation is complete, and a suspect has been charged.

In addition to workload, a concern with appointed counsel is that you do not get to choose your attorney, and there is often a wide range of experience and ability among these attorneys. Some public defenders are experienced and committed professionals, while others are recent law school graduates with no experience. With appointed counsel, the concern is similar. Many young attorneys are willing to take on court-appointed cases because their practice is small, and they are trying to grow their business. A final aspect of relying on appointed counsel that is not always openly discussed is the financial incentives that face public defenders and appointed counsel. Public defenders do not get paid overtime to work additional hours or weekends to prepare for a case. Similarly, in many counties court-appointed counsel are paid a set contract rate regardless of whether a case is resolved with a guilty plea or goes to trial. Under this structure there can be an incentive for the defense attorney and even a fundamental assumption that the vast majority of cases will require very little time and effort and will result in a quick guilty plea.

Those who are not eligible for free counsel or desire to choose their attorney have the right to hire a private attorney. In order to be able to practice in criminal courts, attorneys are only required to have a current license to practice law; they do not have to have any experience, specialized training, or other qualifications.

In order to take full advantage of their right to an attorney, defendants must be willing to ask their appointed counsel about their training, experience, and availability. It is critical that they know who is representing them and how much actual courtroom experience they have. Have they ever tried a criminal case in front of a jury? What were the charges?

You should never be afraid to ask blunt and specific questions about the experience and ability of an attorney. The same applies when it comes to hiring a private attorney.

When hiring a private attorney, you should make sure you understand that attorney's specific experience, not just years of practice—but actual time in the courtroom trying cases in front of a jury. There are many attorneys that are willing to represent clients in a criminal case, for the right price, but that does not mean they have the right experience or strategy for your case.

A few simple questions can help identify the attorneys with the kind of experience that makes a critical difference.

- How long have they been practicing criminal law?

- Where did they go to law school?

- Do they have specific training in trial advocacy?

- Have they received any awards or been recognized for their expertise in litigation or criminal defense?

- Have they ever been a prosecutor?

- Do they base their fees on one flat rate, or is the fee different for a guilty plea versus a trial?

- What continuing legal education on criminal law and trial advocacy do they do to ensure they are current and understand the recent changes in criminal law?

- Do they know the judge, and have they practiced before the judge in the past?

- Do they know the county and understand the types of jurors that will be selected in the location where the case will be tried?

- Do they have the right experience, presence, and skill to be credible in front of the jury?

- Do they have a team of experts and investigators they work with?

- Have they successfully defended multiple defendants facing the same or similar charges?

This list of questions is not exhaustive but should provide a great start for interviewing any attorney you consider hiring. The final question I always recommend asking is whether or not the attorney will guarantee an acquittal. I admit that is a bit of a trick question, but it will tell you whether not the attorney is simply trying to sell themselves or if they are honest and ethical. No attorney can ever guarantee a specific outcome in any case that goes to trial. Any attorney who does, is someone who simply cannot be trusted.[6]

Anyone facing prosecution in the criminal justice system is at risk of losing their future and potentially their freedom. It is critical that you understand your rights. You have the right to remain silent and the right to represented by a competent and capable attorney. You should not waive these rights without fully understanding your rights and the potential consequences.

---

[6] In the book, *ABA Guide to Resolving Legal Disputes: Inside and Outside the Courtroom,* published in the 2009 by the American Bar Association, the authors note that you should, "[b]eware of any lawyer who . . . assures a victory in court." Diversified Publishing 2009.

Chapter 3

How Are You Charged with a Crime in Pennsylvania?

If I am suspected of a crime, how will I find out? Will I know I am under investigation? Who decides if I am going to be charged?

The legal authority to prosecute is referred to as jurisdiction. Pennsylvania has jurisdiction to prosecute criminal activity that occurs within the state. Normally, the investigation and prosecution will be handled by the county where the criminal activity occurred or was discovered.[7]

A law enforcement investigation will begin based on suspicion that criminal activity has occurred or based on

---

[7] As a general rule, the subject matter jurisdiction of criminal courts extends only to offenses committed within the county of trial. *Commonwealth ex rel. Chatary v. Nailon,* 206 A.2d 43 (1965); *Commonwealth v. Frank,* 398 A.2d 663 (1979); *Commonwealth v. Tumolo,* 299 A.2d 15 (1972); *Commonwealth v. Simeone,* 294 A.2d 921 (1972).

the report of criminal activity. A suspect may not know that they are under investigation unless they are confronted and questioned by police at a crime scene. This means that the nature and type of crime will often determine how soon a suspect becomes aware of the investigation.

If a police officer observes what they perceive may be criminal activity, such as in most cases involving driving under the influence of alcohol, an investigation may begin immediately. Alternatively, many other cases are initiated by a witness making a report as the crime is occurring or law enforcement discovery after the crime occurred, as in many burglary cases.

How early in the investigation a suspect will become aware that the investigation is ongoing will also depend on the competence of the investigators and the nature of the investigation. Inexperienced investigators may tip their hand early in the process by forgetting to tell potential witnesses not to talk about the case, or by openly interviewing other witnesses in public areas. These actions can make it obvious an investigation is ongoing. In other serious investigations law enforcement may take significant steps to keep the investigation a secret while they attempt to gather evidence.

Ultimately, you may have no idea you are under investigation until you receive a phone call and are asked to come down to the station or you are served with an arrest warrant and taken into custody. How this will happen is dependent on the case and the circumstances. In cases where there is not a perceived risk of a suspect going into hiding or violence, the police will ask a suspect to come in voluntarily for questioning. In more serious cases or where the police perceive a risk of flight, they can seek an arrest warrant and take a suspect into custody.

The critical point is that often you will not know you are under investigation or a suspect until you are questioned by police. Law enforcement typically calls this a suspect "interview," but it is truly an interrogation designed solely for the purpose of obtaining a confession or incriminating information. Many investigators prefer that a suspect is surprised and taken completely off guard by questioning.

Remember, if you are called in for questioning, investigators are taught to use lies and psychological manipulation techniques during interrogations and interviews in order to obtain "confessions." Many investigators were trained in and still use interrogation techniques that are known to result in false information and false confessions. This training is based on "The Reid Technique," which has been repeatedly shown to result in false confessions.[8] The technique

---

[8] *The Interview – Do police interrogation techniques produce false confessions?* By Douglas Starr, December 9, 2013 Issue, The New Yorker.

involves a carefully orchestrated process designed to convince (through lies and manipulation) the individual being interrogated that they really have no choice other than to confess and that the investigator can help them if they will just admit to what they did. Although people not involved in the criminal justice system are often skeptical of the idea that someone would confess to a crime they did not commit, this technique has been demonstrated repeatedly to result in false confessions.

Regardless of whether you make a statement to law enforcement, the decision to bring charges is made by law enforcement in consultation with the District Attorney's office. Practically, this means that when the investigators believe they have enough evidence (probable cause) to support an arrest, they will present the evidence to an assistant district attorney who will either agree or disagree with the decision to bring charges. When discussing these charging decisions, it is critical to note that law enforcement investigators may have limitations related to their experience, training, policy, and resources that tend to hinder full and fair investigations. Anyone under investigation must understand this reality as they prepare their defense. Just because you are innocent, you cannot blindly trust law enforcement to get it right. In fact, far too often their focus is simply on gathering enough incriminating evidence to substantiate their case and they ignore evidence of innocence.

Politics can also play a significant role in charging decisions. District Attorneys are elected officials, and many face political pressure to prosecute certain types of cases but not others depending on the changing tide of public opinion and media coverage of criminal activity. I have personally been involved in cases that I believe would not have been charged the way they were if the district attorney was not trying to win an election.

If you accept the reality that there are factors that impact and influence criminal investigations and flaws within the charging process that are not related to an unbiased search for the truth and justice, you are in a better position to understand how and why innocent people are charged with crimes. In addition, coming to grips with this reality can help you work effectively with an attorney to protect yourself from bad investigations and work with your defense team to gather exculpatory evidence that may be missed by investigators or ignored by a district attorney.

Chapter 4

Will I Be Arrested and Go to Jail Before my Trial?

One of the most important and life-impacting questions I am asked by anyone who is under investigation or facing possible charges is related to whether or not they will be arrested and put in jail while they await trial. The answer is always case-specific and based on individual facts and circumstances, but the good news is that there are several options available for you to secure pre-trial release so that you do not have to sit in jail before your trial. This chapter outlines the process and discusses the options.

What Happens if I Am Arrested?

In Pennsylvania, an individual charged with a crime is presented with a warrant for their arrest, assuming they are not arrested at the location of the alleged crime or considered a flight risk. How a suspect is presented with the warrant depends on the case and the nature of the charges.

Practices tend to vary between counties, but as a general rule, defendants facing misdemeanor charges will receive their charges in the mail, along with a summons requiring them to appear at a preliminary hearing. Such defendants are generally not a flight risk, nor do they pose a serious threat to the community. Therefore, magisterial district judges will usually set bail at "ROR" or "unsecured" in such cases, at the time the defendant appears for a preliminary hearing. ROR stands for "released on own recognizance," which means that a defendant must simply promise to appear at all future court dates. Unsecured bail does not require a defendant to post any cash to stay out of jail; however, if a defendant on unsecured bail fails to appear at a future court date, then they could be ordered by the court to pay the amount of the unsecured bail when they are apprehended.

There are some misdemeanor cases, where the police will take a defendant into custody for immediate arraignment before a magisterial district judge. For example, if a defendant is homeless, or is planning to leave Pennsylvania or the country, the police may deem the suspect to be too great of a flight risk for them to merely send the summons in the mail. In these cases, because this defendant has no ties to the community, the police may hold them for up to 24-hours until arraignment in order to seek the imposition of cash bail in an amount deemed sufficient to secure the defendant's appearance in court.

In felony cases, the police typically obtain an arrest warrant and take the defendant into custody rather than sending a summons in the mail. The defendant is then taken before the magisterial district judge, where bail is set. If the arrest occurs in the middle of the night, then the defendant will likely be held at the county jail until early the next morning, at which time they will meet with the on-duty magisterial district judge for an informal arraignment. Bail is set at that time.

If felony charges arise from an ongoing investigation that the defendant is aware of and if they have an attorney, the detective will inform the defendant's attorney when charges will be filed. The defense attorney, detective, and magisterial district court will then set a date and time for the defendant to turn themselves in at the magisterial district court. This is known as a "walk-in arrest" or "arrest by appointment." Bail will normally be far less in these cases than when a defendant is simply arrested by surprise and taken into custody. The reason for this difference makes sense. If the defendant has hired an attorney, and voluntarily appeared for the arrest, that is evidence that they will appear for later court proceedings.

Regardless of how the arrest is made, within a 24-hour period after their arrest, anyone who has been charged will be brought before an informal arraignment court judge (typically a magisterial district justice) who will determine whether to set bail, bond or other pre-trial release conditions based on the charges as well as other factors such as the defendant's criminal history, employment status, and ties to the local community.

After the informal arraignment, an initial preliminary hearing date will be set, and the individual charged with the crime will be taken to jail or released with a copy of the written notice to appear for the preliminary hearing.

What Is Bail, and How Is it Set?

The judicial officer conducting the informal arraignment will evaluate the charges and other relevant facts to determine what amount of bail is necessary to secure a defendant's appearance at later proceedings. Under the Pa.R.Crim.P., bail is defined as, "the security or other guarantee required and given for the release of a person, conditioned upon a written undertaking, in the form of a bail bond, that the person will appear when required and comply with all conditions set forth in the bail bond."

Bail is set in all misdemeanor and felony cases, except that a defendant is not entitled to bail if he is charged with an offense punishable by death or life in prison. In some non-homicide cases, a magisterial district court could refuse to set bail if the state demonstrates that pre-trial detention is the only means of securing a defendant's appearance and the district justice agrees.

When setting the type and amount of bail, the district justice will evaluate several legal factors and often some practical ones. These factors include the defendant's likelihood to appear in court and whether they pose a danger to public safety. In making this determination, the district justice will want to know whether the defendant has ever failed to appear in court before, whether the defendant has strong ties to the local community (such as a job and a family), and how much money the defendant has available for bail.

If a judge sets cash bail, the defendant can be released from detention in county jail when someone posts that amount on the defendant's behalf. The person posting bail is known as the "surety." In some cases, the judge may allow the defendant to post only 5% or 10% of the total bail amount. Often, defendants with limited funds will enlist the aid of a bail bondsman, who will post the entire bail amount on the defendant's behalf. The bail bondsman's fee is a percentage of the bail amount. Because this is the bondsman's fee, the person paying the bondsman never gets this money back. If, on the other hand, a friend or family member posts bail, then he or she will get all of the money back after the defendant has either been found not guilty or sentenced.

The judge may also impose non-monetary bail conditions. For example, the judge will always mandate that a defendant have no contact with any potential victims or complaining witnesses and to commit no new violations of law. Another common non-monetary bail condition is that a defendant refrains from using drugs and consuming alcohol. The defendant may also be required to report regularly to the Probation Department or a Bail Agency for "supervised bail." Supervised bail usually includes drug testing. If a defendant violates a non-monetary bail condition, they can expect their bail to be revoked, and they will sit in the county jail until a final order is entered in their case.

What Is Release on Own Recognizance (ROR), and I Will I Be Eligible for It?

ROR is a common tool used in Pennsylvania for misdemeanors and some felony cases. The best way to ensure that

ROR will be deemed appropriate in your case is to ensure that the magistrate has an accurate understanding of the facts and circumstances of your case. If you can demonstrate that you have steady employment, a safe place to live, and significant ties (family, friends, and employment) to the local community, you will be deemed a lower flight and safety risk. In addition, your criminal history will play a significant factor in this decision. If a district justice cannot be convinced that ROR is appropriate, the next best option for most defendants is unsecured bail. Because the bail is unsecured, a defendant does not have to post a bond or make any payments to secure their release, but if they fail to appear at any court proceedings they will be required to pay the full amount of the bail.

So . . . Will I Be Arrested or Put in Jail before I Go to Trial?

It is important to know that in the majority of cases you have the right to have bail set, and you will not be forced to sit in a county jail while you are pending trial. You should work closely with an attorney to establish an arrest by appointment whenever possible. If you are not granted bail or are subject to pre-trial confinement, your attorney can petition the court to reduce the bail, modify non-monetary conditions, and even secure your release.

Chapter 5

What Is a Preliminary Hearing?

Unlike many other states, a defendant in Pennsylvania is usually entitled to a preliminary hearing before their charges are "held over" for trial at the county court of common pleas. The purpose of a preliminary hearing is for a magisterial district justice to hear testimony and review evidence to determine if the Commonwealth can establish a *prima facie* case. *Prima facie* literally means at first appearance. Practically, it means that the magistrate will review the Commonwealth's evidence to determine if there is evidence that would cause a reasonable person to believe a crime occurred and that absent evidence to the contrary, it is more likely than not, the defendant committed the crime.

At the preliminary hearing, the Commonwealth, through a representative from the District Attorney's office, is required to call witnesses to establish the *prima facie* case. If the magistrate rules that the burden is met, then the case will be "held over," which means the charges will be forwarded to the county court of common pleas for trial.

Importantly, what makes this process unique is that defense counsel has the ability to confront and cross-examine witnesses at this hearing. This allows them to assess the witnesses' truthfulness and ability to testify credibly at a later trial. It is also an opportunity to learn about and better understand the strategy the prosecution might use at trial. Most experienced attorneys will hire a court-certified transcriptionist for the hearing or will make a digital recording of the hearing that can be transcribed later.

Regardless of whether or not you are innocent or believe that no reasonable person could conclude you committed a crime, it is critical that you have representation at a preliminary hearing. Not only can the statements you make at the hearing be used against you, it may be critical for your defense and trial strategy that your attorney has an opportunity to observe the testimony of critical witnesses.

Aside from the legal and procedural aspects of the preliminary hearing, it can be just as important to understand what actually happens at most preliminary hearings.

The preliminary hearing usually presents a defense attorney with the first opportunity to speak with the arresting police officer and the Assistant District Attorney that is assigned to the hearing. This initial meeting can be critical because there are times that an effective defense attorney can resolve the case at this stage of the process. Even if the case cannot be dismissed or handled as a summary offense or low-level misdemeanor that can be resolved by the district justice, this initial meeting can help shape the outcome of the case as well as possible plea deal negotiations.

Note, it is very common for defense attorneys to advise their clients to waive the hearing in exchange for some concession from the Commonwealth. In many counties, the DA will have an unwritten policy that if you waive the preliminary hearing, they will make concessions in plea negotiations. It is also common for counties to require a waiver of the preliminary hearing in order to maintain eligibility for pre-trial diversion programs like ARD.

The right to a preliminary hearing is an important part of the criminal process. It is critical to have a clear strategy for what you hope to accomplish at the hearing and that you work closely with your defense team to develop a game plan for the hearing.

Chapter 6

Can First Time Offenders Avoid Jail Time and a Conviction?

Pennsylvania has developed a "pre-trial diversion program" called Accelerated Rehabilitative Disposition (ARD). Programs like ARD are referred to as pre-trial diversion programs because the object is to divert the case from going to trial.

In practice, ARD is a program designed to allow individuals charged with non-violent crimes who have limited or no criminal history to avoid going to trial or facing jail time. In addition, if a defendant successfully completes the requirements of an ARD program, their record will be expungement, and they will not have a criminal conviction on their record.

The stated purpose of the program is the rehabilitation of the offender. Counties have an incentive to use the program because it allows from the prompt disposition of charges, eliminating the need for costly and time-consuming trials or other court proceedings. In order to be accepted into an ARD program defendants are required to waive certain rights in exchange for consideration of their case for ARD. Many counties require a defendant to waive their preliminary hearing, and all counties will require a waiver of the defendant's right to a speedy trial.

Individuals will be accepted into an ARD program if they are believed to be a strong candidate for rehabilitation and if the district attorney's office believes they are not at risk for becoming a repeat offender or that intervention now can prevent future criminal activity. Candidates are carefully screened by the district attorney's office, and a detailed list of requirements and restrictions will be sought based on the nature of the charges. These requirements and restrictions will be negotiated between the district attorney's office and the defendant's attorney. If it is determined they are eligible for and a good candidate, a defendant will be required to agree to the negotiated requirements and restrictions.

Typical requirements include:

- Payment of restitution to any victims;
- Successful completion of substance abuse treatment;
- Periodic drug testing;
- Completion of community service; and
- Obtaining or maintaining employment.

While in the program, defendants are placed under the supervision of the county, similar to being on probation.

One aspect of ARD that defendants need to understand and prepare for are the associated costs. Each county establishes their own costs for entry into the program and can even set higher costs depending on the type of crimes involved. The initial costs of entry into an ARD program can be in excess of $1,500. The costs and fees are intended to pay for the costs of supervision while an individual is in program. The majority of individuals in the ARD program have been arrested for driving under the influence of alcohol or a controlled substance. ARD is also commonly used in low-level drug cases.

The maximum period of supervision for someone on ARD is two years. After successfully completing the program, the ARD offender may petition the court to have the charges dismissed and the case expunged.

Alternatively, if the defendant does not successfully complete the program, the charges will not be dismissed, and the record will not be expunged. Further, they may be removed from the program and have their case listed for trial.

The ARD program is an excellent way, especially for first-time offenders, to avoid criminal trial and the possibility of jail time. Their attorney can help them negotiate a program that they will be able to complete successfully and that ensures any underlying addictions or issues with substance abuse are addressed so they can be rehabilitated. Although there are significant advantages to the program, applying for it is an important decision that should not be taken lightly. Not only do you give up important rights, but successful completion of program will involve a significant investment of time and money. Failure in the program can result in a harsher sentence that includes significant jail time because many judges are hesitant to give a probationary sentence to individuals that are not successful in ARD. Those harsher sentences are based on the belief that the defendant violated a trust and that jail time is necessary to prevent future criminal activity.

Chapter 7

What Happens When Charges Are "Held Over"?

One of the strange legal phrases that is often misunderstood in Pennsylvania's criminal justice system is the statement that charges are being "held over." This is the terminology that is used to describe the transfer of a case from the district justice to the county court of common pleas. This would occur after a preliminary hearing, if the magistrate determined there was sufficient evidence for the case to go to trial. This transfer is a significant event in your case because once the case is transferred, important legal events begin to happen quickly.

Except for those cases that are ARD eligible, the next step in a case that is "held over" is called the filing of the information by the District Attorney's office. This happens primarily behind the scenes as it is simply the process of the

DA formally notifying the county court of the charges and putting them on the record. After the information is filed, formal arraignment will be scheduled.

Formal arraignment is the process where a defendant is formally notified of the charges against them and notified of their basic legal rights.[9] In order to meet the requirements of the law, the formal arraignment process must be sufficient to ensure that a defendant understands they have the right to be represented by counsel; the nature of the charges

---

[9] Pa.R.Crim.P. 571. Arraignment.
   (A) Except as otherwise provided in paragraph (D), arraignment shall be in such form and manner as provided by local court rule. Notice of arraignment shall be given to the defendant as provided in Rule 114 or by first class mail. Unless otherwise provided by local court rule, or postponed by the court for cause shown, arraignment shall take place no later than 10 days after the information has been filed.
   (B) In the discretion of the court, the arraignment of the defendant may be conducted by using two-way simultaneous audio-visual communication. When the counsel for the defendant is present, the defendant must be permitted to communicate fully and confidentially with defense counsel immediately prior to and during the arraignment.
   (C) At arraignment, the defendant shall be advised:
       (1) of the right to be represented by counsel;
       (2) of the nature of the charges contained in the information;
       (3) of the right to file motions, including a Request for a Bill of Particulars, a Motion for Pretrial Discovery and Inspection, a Motion Requesting Transfer from Criminal Proceedings to Juvenile Proceedings Pursuant to 42 Pa.C.S. § 6322, and an Omnibus Pretrial Motion, and the time limits within which the motions must be filed; and.
       (4) if the defendant fails to appear without cause at any proceeding for which the defendant's presence is required, including trial, that the defendant's absence may be deemed a waiver of the right to be present, and the proceeding may be conducted in the defendant's absence. If the defendant or counsel has not received a copy of the information(s) pursuant to Rule 562, a copy thereof shall be provided.
   (D) A defendant may waive appearance at arraignment if the following requirements are met:
       (1) the defendant is represented by counsel of record and counsel concurs in the waiver; and
       (2) the defendant and counsel sign and file with the clerk of courts a waiver of appearance at arraignment that acknowledges the defendant:
           (a) understands the nature of the charges;
           (b) understands the rights and requirements contained in paragraph (C) of this rule; and
           (c) waives his or her right to appear for arraignment.

against them; their right to file motions; (including a Request for a Bill of Particulars) a Motion for Pretrial Discovery and Inspection, a Motion Requesting Transfer from Criminal Proceedings to Juvenile Proceedings Pursuant to 42 Pa.C.S. § 6322, and an Omnibus Pretrial Motion; and the time limits within which the motions must be filed. Also, once formal arraignment has occurred, if a defendant fails to appear without cause at any trial proceeding after that, including trial, the defendant's absence may be deemed a waiver of the right to be present, and the proceeding may be conducted without the defendant. While this is rare, it is worth noting as significant because the right to be present and trial and other trial proceedings is an important constitutional right.

After the arraignment, a defendant and their attorney typically have 30 days to file any necessary motions related to the case. The most common motions include motions to compel discovery (a request to force the prosecutor to produce evidence that is relevant to the case) and motions to suppress evidence (a request that the judge prevent the prosecution from presenting evidence at trial that was obtained as the product of an illegal act by law enforcement such as an unlawful search or seizure or a statement taken without notifying a suspect of their right to remain silent and consult with an attorney).

If motions are filed in a case, the judge will schedule a motions hearing to allow both sides to present evidence and make legal arguments. Once motions hearings are complete, the case will be listed for trial.

Listing a case for trial literally means that a case will be put on the list of cases that may go to trial during a given trial term. Trial terms are established by the chief judge for each county and typically last one to two weeks. Depending on the county, just because a case is listed for trial during a specific trial term does not mean trial will happen during that term.

When a case goes to trial will be based on the availability of witnesses, attorneys, and the availability of the judge. Another factor in timing relates to the number of cases on the trial list and the placement of a case on the trial list. In many counties, the district attorney's office will determine where a case is placed on the trial list based on the priority, they assign the case. There are many factors that go into the placement, but typically cases are prioritized based on how long trial has pending and the availability of witnesses.

When your case is transferred or "held over" to the county court of common pleas, it is critical that you understand the next steps in the process and that you work closely with your defense team to ensure that your rights are protected at each stage of the process. You should never waive any rights or just assume that any aspect of the handling of your case is normal or typical. You should ask questions and ensure that you understand how quickly your case will move from formal arraignment to the trial list so that you and your attorney are fully prepared for trial.

Chapter 8

Should I Take a Plea Deal?

The decision to accept a plea bargain in your case is deeply personal, highly specific to the facts and circumstances of your case, and one that should never be entered into lightly. Any criminal conviction can have significant lifelong consequences and making the decision to plead guilty in any case a difficult one. Not only should anyone considering pleading guilty do so because they will receive a better sentence if they do, but they must also truly be prepared and understand the consequences of a criminal conviction. A felony conviction can significantly impact your ability to get a job, take away your right to vote, and impact your ability to own a gun. Any conviction involving a sexual offense can result in sex offender registration and reporting requirements that can impact where you are allowed to live and work. Many misdemeanor convictions also have significant lifelong consequences. No one should ever accept a plea deal or plead guilty unless they fully and completely understand all of the implications of their guilty plea and fully discuss them with their attorney.

If a defendant is considering pleading guilty or taking a deal, the place to start should always be whether or not the defendant believes they are guilty. If someone is not guilty of a charged offense, they should be working with their attorney to have the charge dropped as part of a plea deal or preparing for trial. The one exception is in rare cases where a defendant is permitted to enter a no-contest plea. In these cases the defendants are not specifically admitting that they are guilty, instead they are stating that they are not going to contest the charge, and regardless of whether they are innocent they believe the prosecution has sufficient evidence to prove the charge at trial. No contest pleas are disfavored by the system because judges expect defendants to accept responsibility for their actions or plead not guilty and go to trial. If a defendant is not guilty but feels it is in their best interest to take a plea deal because of their belief that they will be convicted if they go to trial, a no-contest plea may be the only reasonable option.

The more common outcome of a plea deal involves the prosecution making concessions based on a defendant's willingness to plead guilty. The concessions might include a specific limitation on a sentence or type of sentence (probation or house arrest rather than jail time) or the reduction or dismissal of specific charges.

The common factors that go into this negotiation are the specifics facts of your case and how difficult it will be for the Commonwealth to prove their case at trial. Politics may also play a role. If there is political pressure to be hard on a particular type of crime, especially if a District Attorney is running for re-election, it can have a significant impact on the negotiations. If there were any victims in the case, the District Attorney's office will seek their input to determine how they feel about a potential plea deal. A defense attorney may ask for additional information from a defendant to aid in these negotiations. For example, character letters, work history, voluntary treatment or counseling, and medical or mental health diagnoses are all factors that may assist in reducing the terms of a plea deal, much as they would in a sentencing hearing. By advocating for these mitigating factors during plea negotiations an experienced attorney may be able to significantly reduce the sentencing terms of the plea deal.

Once the negotiations are complete and the final offer is presented, the decision to accept the plea deal often comes down to a careful analysis of the risks of going to trial versus the rewards of the negotiated plea deal. If a plea deal significantly reduces the potential sentence a defendant might receive if convicted of all charges, then it may be in their best interest to plead guilty. They should also consider the potential that the sentencing judge may impose a "trial tax" if they plead not guilty. A so-called "trial tax" is when a judge imposes a significantly harsher sentence for the same crime after a trial than they normally impose if there is a guilty plea. This sentencing disparity is often justified legally by the contention that pleading guilty is a sign of remorse and a factor to be considered in evaluating rehabilitation potential.

Remember, you have the absolute right to a trial by jury, and no one can force you to plead guilty or take a plea deal. The decision of whether or not to plead guilty should only be made after full consultation with your attorney and if you understand all of the consequences of a conviction and the potential sentence.

Chapter 9

How Are Juries Selected in Pennsylvania?

The rules governing the qualification, selection, and summoning of prospective jurors, as well as related matters, are generally dealt with in Chapter 45, Subchapters A–C, of the Pennsylvania Judicial Code.[10] Pursuant to the Judicial Code, anyone who is facing a jury trial has the right to jurors selected at random from a representative cross-section of the eligible population of the county. Further, the Code requires that all qualified citizens have the opportunity to be considered for service as jurors...and have an obligation to serve as jurors when summoned for jury duty. Finally, the Code prohibits the exclusion of a citizen from serving as a juror on the basis of

---

[10] 42 Pa.C.S. §§ 4501 – 4503, 4521 – 4526, and 4531 – 4532.

race, color, religion, sex, national origin, or economic status. A citizen is considered qualified for jury duty if they are old enough to vote; can read, write, speak, and understand the English language; and if they have not been convicted of a crime punishable by imprisonment for more than one year. At a minimum, the list of potential jurors will include all registered voters of a county. Each county is required to establish a commission that maintains the list of potential jurors and selects at random a master list of prospective jurors for jury service. The number of potential jurors selected is designated by the presiding judge for the county. Once the master list of randomly selected jurors is complete each of the selected jurors is sent a notice and a jury qualification form that is used to determine whether a potential juror is qualified. Once the master list of qualified jurors is final for a trial term, an "array" (group of potential jurors) will be assigned to a specific case. It is from this array of twenty-five to one hundred potential jurors that a jury of twelve members and typically two alternates are selected for a specific case.

Once the array for a specific case is established, the prosecuting attorney and the defense attorney are provided a written jury questionnaire completed by each potential juror. These questionnaires provide basic information from a standard list of questions that includes basic biographical data, education, job history, and other general information about a potential juror.[11] What follows is a copy of the standard questionnaire.

JUROR INFORMATION QUESTIONNAIRE
CONFIDENTIAL; NOT PUBLIC RECORD

File # __________

NAME: Last	First	Middle Initial

City/Township	Communities in which you resided over the past 10 years:	

Marital Status		Number of Children

Occupation	Occupation(s) past 10 years	
Occupation of Spouse/Other	Past 10 years occupation of spouse/other	

RACE

Levels of Education: Yours	Spouse/Other	Children

1. Have you ever served as a juror before? ……………………………………………………………
   If so, were you ever on a hung jury? ……………………………………………………………………
2. Do you have any religious, moral or ethical beliefs that would prevent you from sitting in judgment in a criminal case and rendering a fair verdict? ………………………………………
3. Do you have any physical or psychological disability that might interfere with or prevent you from serving as a juror? …………………………………………………………………………
4. Have you or anyone close to you ever been the victim of a crime? ………………………………
5. Have you or anyone close to you ever been charged with or arrested for a crime, other than a traffic violation? …………………………………………………………………………………
6. Have you or anyone close to you ever been an eyewitness to a crime, whether or not it ever came to court? ………………………………………………………………………………………
7. Have you or anyone close to you ever worked in law enforcement or the justice system? This includes police, prosecutors, attorneys, detectives, security or prison guards, and court related agencies. ……………………………………………………………………………………
8. Would you be more likely to believe the testimony of a police officer or any other law enforcement officer because of his or her job? ……………………………………………………
9. Would you be less likely to believe the testimony of a police officer or any other law enforcement officer because of his or her job? ……………………………………………………
10. Would you have any problem following the court's instruction that the defendant in a criminal case is presumed to be innocent unless and until proven guilty beyond a reasonable doubt? …………
11. Would you have any problem following the court's instruction that the defendant in a criminal case does not have to take the stand or present evidence, and it cannot be held against the defendant if he or she elects to remain silent or present no evidence? ……………………………
12. Would you have any problem following the court's instruction in a criminal case that just because someone is arrested, it does not mean that the person is guilty of anything? ………………………
13. In general, would you have any problem following and applying the judge's instruction on the law?
14. Would you have any problem during jury deliberations in a criminal case discussing the case fully but still making up your own mind? …………………………………………………………………
15. Are you presently taking any medication that might interfere with or prevent you from serving as a juror? …………………………………………………………………………………………………
16. Is there any other reason you could not be a fair juror in a criminal case? ………………………

I hereby certify that the answers on this form are true and correct. I understand that false answers provided herein subject me to penalties under 18 Pa.C.S. § 4904 relating to unsworn falsification to authorities.

Signature:________________________________Date: __________

PLEASE COMPLETE AND RETURN WITHIN 5 DAYS TO:
COURT ADMINISTRATOR

---

[11] The required form of the juror information questionnaire is established by Pa.R.Crim.P. 632.

After the attorneys have had the opportunity to review the questionnaires, the array is brought into the courtroom, informed of the name of the defendant and the general nature of the case. Once that process is complete, the judge will ask a series of general questions to ensure that the potential jurors are qualified to serve, and then the prosecuting attorney and the defense attorney have the opportunity to question the potential jurors. Once the questioning (also called *voir dire* which is French for to speak the truth), is complete, the prosecution and defense have the opportunity to challenge any potential juror "for cause." For cause means that there is a reason or cause to believe that the juror is not qualified to serve as a juror or that they cannot be fair and impartial in a particular case.[12]

---

[12] Pa.R.Crim.P. 631. Examination and Challenges of Trial Jurors.

    (A) Voir dire of prospective trial jurors and prospective alternate jurors shall be conducted, and the jurors shall be selected, in the presence of a judge, unless the judge's presence is waived by the attorney for the Commonwealth, the defense attorney, and the defendant, with the judge's consent.

    (B) This oath shall be administered individually or collectively to the prospective jurors: "You do solemnly swear by Almighty God (or do declare and affirm) that you will answer truthfully all questions that may be put to you concerning your qualifications for service as a juror."

    (C) Upon completion of the oath, the judge shall instruct the prospective jurors upon their duties and restrictions while serving as jurors, and of any sanctions for violation of those duties and restrictions, including those provided in Rule 626(C) and Rule 627.

    (D) Voir dire, including the judge's ruling on all proposed questions, shall be recorded in full unless the recording is waived. The record will be transcribed only upon written request of either party or order of the judge.

    (E) Prior to voir dire, each prospective juror shall complete the standard, confidential juror information questionnaire as provided in Rule 632. The judge may require the parties to submit in writing a list of proposed questions to be asked of the jurors regarding their qualifications. The judge may permit the defense and the prosecution to conduct the examination of prospective jurors or the judge may conduct the examination. In the latter event, the judge shall permit

The judge decides whether a potential juror should be excused for cause. After the for cause process is complete, each side has the opportunity to exercise peremptory challenges. When a peremptory challenge is made, the attorney does not have to provide any reason or justification for the challenge, and exercising the challenge means that the juror they identify is removed from the array and does not serve on the case. The number of peremptory challenges each side has to exercise is determined by the type of case, including whether the charges involve a felony and the number of co-defendants.[13] The only limitation on the exercise of

---

the defense and the prosecution to supplement the examination by such further inquiry as the judge deems proper.

(F) In capital cases, the individual voir dire method must be used, unless the defendant waives that alternative.

[13] Pa.R.Crim.P. 634. Number of Peremptory Challenges.

(A) Trials involving only one defendant:

    (1) In trials involving misdemeanors only and when there is only one defendant, the commonwealth and the defendant shall each be entitled to 5 peremptory challenges.

    (2) In trials involving a non-capital felony and when there is only one defendant, the commonwealth and the defendant shall each be entitled to 7 peremptory challenges.

    (3) In trials involving a capital felony and when there is only one defendant, the commonwealth and the defendant shall each be entitled to 20 peremptory challenges.

(B) Trials involving joint defendants:

    (1) In trials involving joint defendants, the defendants shall divide equally among them that number of peremptory challenges that the defendant charged with the highest grade of offense would have received if tried separately; provided, however, that each defendant shall be entitled to at least 2 peremptory challenges. When such division of peremptory challenges among joint defendants results in a fraction of a peremptory challenge, each defendant shall be entitled to the next highest number of such challenges.

    (2) In trials involving joint defendants, it shall be within the discretion of the trial judge to increase the number of peremptory challenges to which each defendant is entitled up to the number of peremptory challenges that each defendant would have received if tried alone.

    (3) In trials involving joint defendants, the commonwealth shall be entitled to peremptory challenges equal in number to the total number of peremptory challenges given to all of the defendants.

peremptory challenges stem from the Equal Protection Clause of the Fourteenth Amendment. The Supreme Court has found that the intentional use of peremptory challenges to remove potential jurors based on their race violated the Fourteenth Amendment.[14]

The jury questioning and selection or *voir dire* process is obviously critical to a positive outcome. You and your defense team need to be prepared to work together to identify jurors with characteristics that are either favorable or unfavorable to your case. In addition to developing a profile of potentially favorable and unfavorable juror characteristics before the process begins, you will need to pay close attention to the reactions and mannerisms of potential jurors in the process. Any juror that appears too eager to serve or completely and totally disinterested is typically dangerous. You may also see personalities come to light during *voir dire.* By carefully observing and noting which potential jurors answer first or quickly and those that look around the room before answering, you can begin to identify individuals that will be leaders during the deliberation process. Ultimately, successful jury selection requires experience, teamwork, and communication. Do not wait until you are sitting in the courtroom to discuss the process with your

---

[14] *Batson v. Kentucky*, 476 U.S. 79 (1986).

attorney! Make sure that you and your defense team have a clear game plan developed before you arrive in court.

Chapter 10

Who Decides My Sentence and What Is the Maximum Punishment?

If you are convicted of any offense, you will be sentenced by a judge. Under the rules, the sentencing judge for your case is the judge that presided over your trial.[15]

As an aid in determining an appropriate sentence, the judge will typically order a Pre-Sentence Investigation

---

[15] Rule 700. Sentencing Judge.

    (A) Except as provided in paragraph (B), the judge who presided at the trial or who received the plea of guilty or nolo contendere shall impose sentence unless there are extraordinary circumstances which preclude the judge's presence. In such event, another judge shall be assigned to impose sentence.

    (B) A court may provide by local rule that sentence on a plea of guilty or nolo contendere may be imposed by a judge other than the judge who received a plea of guilty or nolo contendere. In such event, the defendant must be so notified at the time of entering the plea.

(PSI).[16] The purpose of the PSI is to provide the judge with additional background information to consider when determining an appropriate sentence. The probation office will conduct the PSI and prepare a report for the judge. The key elements of the report include the defendant's criminal history, family and marital history, health (physical and mental), education, employment, and input from any potential victims.

How Will a Judge Determine What Sentence Is Appropriate in My Case?

After the completion of the PSI the judge will arrive at a sentence based on the consideration of several factors, including the sentencing guidelines. Judges are required to balance public safety, the impact of the crime on the victim and the community, and the rehabilitation of the defendant.

---

[16] Rule 702. Aids in Imposing Sentence.
  (A) PRE-SENTENCE INVESTIGATION REPORT.
    (1) The sentencing judge may, in the judge's discretion, order a pre-sentence investigation report in any case.
    (2) The sentencing judge shall place on the record the reasons for dispensing with the pre-sentence investigation report if the judge fails to order a pre-sentence report in any of the following instances:
      (a) when incarceration for one year or more is a possible disposition under the applicable sentencing statutes;
      (b) when the defendant is less than 21 years old at the time of conviction or entry of a plea of guilty; or
      (c) when a defendant is a first offender in that he or she has not heretofore been sentenced as an adult.
    (3) The pre-sentence investigation report shall include information regarding the circumstances of the offense and the character of the defendant sufficient to assist the judge in determining sentence.
    (4) The pre-sentence investigation report shall also include a victim impact statement as provided by law.

The judge must also consider the sentencing guidelines set forth by the Pennsylvania Commission on Sentencing. The guidelines provide a possible range of sentences for the judge to consider in arriving at a sentence.

Once the guideline range has been determined, the judge will then decide on a specific punishment based on any mitigating or aggravating factors in the defendant's case.

Mitigating factors include evidence that reflects positively on the defendant and should be used to argue for a shorter sentence. Typical mitigating factors include cooperating with the police, a record of consistent employment, a supportive family, pleading guilty, attempts by the defendant to further their education, a showing of genuine remorse, and limited or no criminal history. Aggravating factors include evidence that reflects poorly on the defendant and may contribute to a longer sentence. These factors generally include a sporadic or non-existent employment history, a history of violence, lack of genuine remorse, and a lengthy criminal record.

Although the guidelines will play a significant role in the judge's decision, judges are not bound by the guidelines and can sentence a defendant outside the guideline range. Because of this discretion, it is critical that every defendant prepare carefully and thoughtfully for sentencing.

One effective tool many experienced attorneys use is called a sentencing memorandum. This is a written legal memorandum that outlines the mitigating factors they believe the judge should consider in the case and will typically be supported with character letters, diplomas, training certificates, and other documents that provide evidentiary support for the mitigating factors.

In addition to working closely with their attorney to prepare a sentencing memorandum, a defendant will have the opportunity to address the judge. Not only what a defendant says, but what they wear, their mannerisms and body language can have a significant impact on the judge.

Every aspect of the statement, including the clothes you wear, should be discussed with your attorney. While it may seem obvious that you should dress appropriately for court, I have seen a defendant show up for sentencing wearing a t-shirt that said, "only God can judge me." In another case, a drug case, I observed a defendant who showed up wearing a t-shirt with a large marijuana leaf that said, "legalize it." Obviously, their attorneys did not discuss their sentencing attire with them, and it is no surprise that things did not go well for them. These kinds of mistakes can be avoided through careful planning and teamwork.

What Is the Maximum Punishment I Am Facing?

In addition to understanding the process, it is important to understand the maximum punishments that are associated with each type or classification of offense. The maximum punishment for an offense is dependent on the classification of the crime. In Pennsylvania, the crime classifications include the following:

- Murder
- First-Degree Felony (F1)
- Second-Degree Felony (F2)
- Third-Degree Felony (F3)
- Ungraded Felony (F)
- First-Degree Misdemeanor (M1)
- Second-Degree Misdemeanor (M2)
- Third-Degree Misdemeanor (M3)
- Ungraded Misdemeanor (M)
- Summary Offenses (S)

Murder

Offenses categorized as murder include murder, murder of an unborn child, murder of a law enforcement officer, and felony murder. Felony murder (charged when someone is killed during the commission of a felony offense such as a robbery) may be categorized as first, second or third-degree.

Murder in the first-degree is a capital offense in Pennsylvania. Capital offenses are crimes that are punishable by death. Murder in the first-degree carries a possible penalty of life in prison or death. Murder in the second-degree and first-degree murder of an unborn child carry a sentence of life in prison.

Murder in the third-degree has a maximum sentence of 40 years in prison. Attempted murder, solicitation to commit murder, or conspiracy to commit murder where serious bodily injury occurs also have a maximum penalty of 40 years in prison. If serious bodily injury does not occur, the maximum penalty for attempted murder, solicitation to commit murder, and conspiracy to commit murder is 20 years in prison.

The age of an offender can impact the maximum punishment as well. First-degree murder committed by a person under the age of 18 does not carry the possibility of a death sentence. A person who is 15 years old or older at the time they commit first-degree murder can be sentenced to a minimum term of 35 years in prison up to a maximum of life imprisonment. A person who is under the age of 15 at the time of committing first-degree murder will be sentenced to a minimum term of 25 years to life in prison.

Felony Offenses

Felony offenses are categorized as Felony Murder, Felony in the first-degree (F1), Felony in the second-degree (F2), Felony in the third-degree (F3), or Ungraded Felony (F), which carries the same punishment limitations as an F3. The degree is based on the how serious the offense is determined to be as determined by statute. The minimum and maximum penalties for a felony conviction depend on the degree.

First-Degree Felonies

The penalties for a first-degree felony conviction include from 10 to 20 years in prison and a fine of up to $25,000. First-degree Felonies include crimes like:

- Felony Murder
- Aggravated assault with a deadly weapon
- Kidnapping
- Rape
- Arson endangering persons
- Theft of property worth $500,000 or more

Second-Degree Felonies

A conviction for a felony in the second-degree in Pennsylvania includes from 5 to 10 years in prison and a fine of up to $25,000. This includes crimes like:

- Sexual assault
- Involuntary manslaughter of a victim under 12 years old
- Burglary (with no one in the structure)
- Indecent assault
- Aggravated assault
- Theft of property worth at least $100,000 but less than $500,000.

Third-Degree Felonies

A conviction for a felony in the third-degree in Pennsylvania includes from 3 1/2 to 7 years in prison and a fine of up to $15,000. This includes crimes like:

- Bribery
- Possession of child pornography
- Possession with intent to distribute
- Certain gun crimes
- Theft of property worth more than $2,000 but less than $100,000

Collateral Consequences of Felony Convictions

Felony convictions carry repercussions that are collateral to and extend beyond the sentence. Even after the sentence is complete, anyone convicted of a felony offense will face the life-long stigma of being a felon and have limitations on their freedom. Regardless of the degree of felony conviction, it is also more difficult for felons to get a job, join the military, find a place to live, and enter certain professions. Specifically, if you have been convicted of a felony in Pennsylvania, you may be prohibited from or have limitations on your ability to:

- Run for public office
- Own or possess a firearm
- Vote
- Serve on a jury
- Obtain college financial aid
- Receive some types of government benefits

Misdemeanors

Misdemeanor crimes are generally less serious than felony offenses; however, they can still result in mandatory minimum prison time and expensive fines. Misdemeanors, like felonies, are divided by degree, from first-degree (M1) to third-degree (M3). Ungraded misdemeanors typically carry the same punishments an M3.

First-Degree Misdemeanors

The penalties for a first-degree misdemeanor conviction include from 2.5 to 5 years in prison and a fine of up to $10,000. This includes crimes like:

- Simple assault
- Terroristic threats
- Stalking
- Assault of a sports official
- Multiple DUI offenses
- Theft of property worth at least $200 but less than $2,000

Second-Degree Misdemeanors

The penalties for a second-degree misdemeanor conviction range from 1 to 2 years in prison and a fine of up to $5,000. Second-degree misdemeanors include crimes like:

- Bigamy
- Shoplifting
- Impersonating a public servant
- Strangulation
- Theft of property worth at least $50 but less than $200

Third-Degree Misdemeanors

The penalties for a third-degree misdemeanor conviction include from 6 months to 1 year in prison and a fine of up to $2,500. Third-degree misdemeanors include crimes like:

- Possession of marijuana
- Open lewdness
- Railroad vandalism
- Loitering and prowling at night
- Theft of property worth less than $50

Summary Offenses

A summary offense is a lesser crime than a felony or misdemeanor. The maximum penalty for a summary offense includes 90 days in jail and a fine of up to $300. In most cases, a conviction for a summary offense will result in a fine but not jail time. Summary offenses are the most common criminal charges in Pennsylvania. They are sometimes referred to as "non-traffic citations." While they generally do not result in jail time, a conviction will result in a criminal record that may have to be disclosed to future employers. Examples of some common summary offenses are:

- Disorderly conduct
- Loitering
- Harassment
- Underage drinking

The Sentencing Matrix

In addition to the classification of an offense, each offense has a statutorily established Offense Grade Score or OGS and a Prior Record Score. The OGS determines the sentencing guideline level of an offense and the corresponding guideline sentencing range. The Prior Record Score is added to the calculation and may result in an increase in the guideline sentencing range. The Prior Record Score will range from 0 for first-time offenders and those with a criminal history that is limited to one or two summary offenses to 5 for repeat offenders. The judge will use the OGS and the Prior Record Score to determine the guideline range using the "Basic Sentencing Matrix." An example is provided on the following page.

No one ever wants to go to jail. However, if you are facing criminal charges, you need to mentally and financially prepare for the possibility of jail time. Even if you are innocent, you cannot control the outcome of a trial. With that in mind, anyone facing the possibility of a criminal conviction must make sure that their families understand that a sentence to jail, while difficult, is something that they can safely endure. They should focus and plan to take full advantage of every training, counseling, and rehabilitative program available. While never easy, many people emerge from their time in prison with increased vocational training, a degree, and with a healthy perspective on the future.

Pennsylvania Commission on Sentencing

§303.16(a). Basic Sentencing Matrix.

7th Edition Amendment 3 (09/25/2015)

Level	OGS	Example Offenses	Prior Record Score								AGG/MIT
			0	1	2	3	4	5	RFEL	REVOC	
LEVEL 5 State Incar	14	Murder 3 Inchoate Murder (SBI) Rape (victim <13 yrs)	72-SL	84-SL	96-SL	120-SL	168-SL	192-SL	204-SL	SL	~/-12
	13	Inchoate Murder (No SBI) Weapons Mass Destr-Use PWID Cocaine (>1,000 g)	60-78	66-84	72-90	78-96	84-102	96-114	108-126	240	+/- 12
	12	Rape-Forcible Compulsion IDSI-Forcible Compulsion Robbery-Inflicts SBI	48-66	54-72	60-78	66-84	72-90	84-102	96-114	120	+/- 12
	11	Agg Assault-Cause SBI Voluntary Manslaughter Sexual Assault PWID Cocaine (100-1,000 g)	36-54 BC	42-60	48-66	54-72	60-78	72-90	84-102	120	+/- 12
	10	Kidnapping Agg Indecent Assault F2 Arson-Person in Building Hom by Vehicle-DUI & Work Zone	22-36 BC	30-42 BC	36-48 BC	42-54	48-60	60-72	72-84	120	+/- 12
	9	Sexual Exploitation of Children Robbery-Commit/Threat F1/F2 Burglary-Home/Person Present Arson-No Person in Building	12-24 BC	18-30 BC	24-36 BC	30-42 BC	36-48 BC	48-60	60-72	120	+/- 12
LEVEL 4 State Incar/ RIP trade	8 (F1)	Agg Assault -Cause BI w/DW Theft (Firearm) Identity theft (3rd/+ & Vic>=60 yrs) Hom by Veh-DUI or Work Zone Theft (>$100,000) PWID Cocaine (10-<50 g)	9-16 BC	12-18 BC	15-21 BC	18-24 BC	21-27 BC	27-33 BC	40-52	NA	+/- 9
LEVEL 3 State/ Cnty Incar RIP trade	7 (F2)	Robbery-Inflicts/Threatens BI Burglary-Home/No Person Present Statutory Sexual Assault Theft (>$50,000-$100,000) Identity Theft (3rd/subq) PWID Cocaine (5-<10 g)	6-14 BC	9-16 BC	12-18 BC	15-21 BC	18-24 BC	24-30 BC	35-45 BC	NA	+/- 6
	6	Agg Assault-Cause Fear of SBI Homicide by Vehicle Burglary-Not a Home/Person Prsnt Theft (>$25,000-$50,000) Arson-Endanger Property PWID Cocaine (2<5 g)	3-12 BC	6-14 BC	9-16 BC	12-18 BC	15-21 BC	21-27 BC	27-40 BC	NA	+/- 6
LEVEL 2 Cnty Incar RIP RS	5 (F3)	Burglary F2 Theft (>$2000-$25,000) Bribery PWID Marij (1-<10 lbs)	RS-9	1-12 BC	3-14 BC	6-16 BC	9-16 BC	12-18 BC	24-36 BC	NA	+/- 3
	4	Indecent Assault M2 Forgery (Money, Stocks) Weapon on School Property Crim Trespass F2	RS-3	RS-9	RS-<12	3-14 BC	6-16 BC	9-16 BC	21-30 BC	NA	+/- 3
	3 (M1)	Simple Assault-Attempt/Cause BI Theft ($200-$2000) Carrying Explosives Simple Possession	RS-1	RS-6	RS-9	RS-<12	3-14 BC	6-16 BC	12-18 BC	NA	+/- 3
LEVEL 1 RS	2 (M2)	Theft ($50-<$200) Retail Theft (1st/2nd Offense) Bad Checks ($500-<$1,000)	RS	RS-2	RS-3	RS-4	RS-6	1-9	6-<12	NA	+/- 3
	1 (M3)	Most Misd. 3's;Theft (<$50) DUI (M) Poss Small Amount Marij	RS	RS-1	RS-2	RS-3	RS-4	RS-6	3-6	NA	+/- 3

1. Designated areas of the matrix indicate restrictive intermediate punishments may be imposed as a substitute for incarceration.

2. When restrictive intermediate punishments are appropriate, the duration of the restrictive intermediate punishment programs are recommended not to exceed the guideline ranges.

3. When the range is RS through a number of months (e.g. RS-6), RIP may be appropriate.

4. All numbers in sentence recommendations suggest months of minimum confinement pursuant to 42 Pa.C.S. 9755(b) and 9756(b).

5. Statutory classification (e.g., F1, F2, etc.) in brackets reflect the omnibus OGS assignment for the given grade.

Key:

BC	=	boot camp
CNTY	=	county
INCAR	=	incarceration
PWID	=	possession with intent to deliver
REVOC	=	repeat violent offender category
RFEL	=	repeat felony 1 and felony 2 offender category
RIP	=	restrictive intermediate punishments
RS	=	restorative sanctions
SBI	=	serious bodily injury
SL	=	statutory limit (longest minimum sentence)
~	=	no recommendation (aggravated sentence would exceed statutory limit)
<; >	=	less than; greater than

Chapter 11

Can I Appeal My Conviction?

If you are convicted, you have the right to appeal the conviction and the sentence. The fight to overturn a wrongful conviction or an unjust sentence has several important stages. Make sure you understand your rights so you can take full advantage of every opportunity to exercise them.

Each phase or important aspect of post-trial processing is addressed in the following pages. The terminology that is used in describing this processing is the terminology that is used by the courts and becoming familiar with the terminology and the timelines is an important part of the effort to

understand the process and ensure your rights are protected.[17]

---

[17] Rule 720. Post-Sentencing Procedures; Appeal.
  (A) TIMING.
    (1) Except as provided in paragraphs (C) and (D), a written post-sentence mo-
tion shall be filed no later than 10 days after imposition of sentence.
    (2) If the defendant files a timely post-sentence motion, the notice of appeal
shall be filed:
      (a) within 30 days of the entry of the order deciding the motion;
      (b) within 30 days of the entry of the order denying the motion by opera-
tion of law in cases in which the judge fails to decide the motion; or
      (c) within 30 days of the entry of the order memorializing the withdrawal
in cases in which the defendant withdraws the motion.
    (3) If the defendant does not file a timely post-sentence motion, the defendant's
notice of appeal shall be filed within 30 days of imposition of sentence, except as provided in paragraph (A)(4).
    (4) If the Commonwealth files a timely motion to modify sentence pursuant to
Rule 721, the defendant's notice of appeal shall be filed within 30 days of
the entry of the order disposing of the Commonwealth's motion.
  (B) OPTIONAL POST-SENTENCE MOTION.
    (1) Generally.
      (a) The defendant in a court case shall have the right to make a post-sen-
tence motion. All requests for relief from the trial court shall be stated
with specificity and particularity, and shall be consolidated in the
post-sentence motion, which may include:
        (i) a motion challenging the validity of a plea of guilty or nolo conten-
dere, or the denial of a motion to withdraw a plea of guilty or nolo
contendere;
        (ii) a motion for judgment of acquittal;
        (iii) a motion in arrest of judgment;
        (iv) a motion for a new trial; and/or
        (v) a motion to modify sentence.
      (b) The defendant may file a supplemental post-sentence motion in the
judge's discretion as long as the decision on the supplemental motion
can be made in compliance with the time limits of paragraph (B)(3).
      (c) Issues raised before or during trial shall be deemed preserved for ap-
peal whether or not the defendant elects to file a post-sentence motion
on those issues.
    (2) Trial Court Action.
      (a) Briefing Schedule
      Within 10 days after a post-sentence motion is filed, if the judge deter-
mines that briefs or memoranda of law are required for a resolution
of the motion, the judge shall schedule a date certain for the submission of briefs or memoranda of law by the defendant and the
Commonwealth.
      (b) Hearing; Argument
      The judge shall also determine whether a hearing or argument on the mo-
tion is required, and if so, shall schedule a date or dates certain for one
or both.
      (c) Transcript
      If the grounds asserted in the post-sentence motion do not require a tran-
script, neither the briefs nor hearing nor argument on the post-
sentence motion shall be delayed for transcript preparation.

Post-Sentencing Memorandum

After sentencing, a defendant has 10 days to file a written post-sentencing memorandum. Failure to file a written post-sentencing memorandum may result in the waiver of certain rights and the inability to raise those matters on appeal. All "requests for relief" from the trial court should be included in the memorandum. What this means is that you are asking the judge to correct what you believe are legal errors that occurred during the trial or sentencing proceedings. Unless it was raised in a motion before or during trial, an error must be raised in the Post-Sentencing Memorandum or it may be deemed waived and your right to raise it on appeal may be forfeited. The motions that are addressed in the memorandum include:

---

(3) Time Limits for Decision on Motion.

    The judge shall not vacate sentence pending decision on the post-sentence motion, but shall decide the motion as provided in this paragraph.

    (a) Except as provided in paragraph (B)(3)(b), the judge shall decide the post-sentence motion, including any supplemental motion, within 120days of the filing of the motion. If the judge fails to decide the motion within 120 days, or to grant an extension as provided in paragraph (B)(3)(b), the motion shall be deemed denied by operation of law.

  (b) Upon motion of the defendant within the 120-day disposition period, for good cause shown, the judge may grant one 30-day extension for decision on the motion. If the judge fails to decide the motion within the 30-day extension period, the motion shall be deemed denied by operation of law.

  (c) When a post-sentence motion is denied by operation of law, the clerk of courts shall forthwith enter an order on behalf of the court, and, as provided in Rule 114, forthwith shall serve a copy of the order on the attorney for the Commonwealth, the defendant's attorney, or the defendant if unrepresented, that the post-sentence motion is deemed denied. This order is not subject to reconsideration.

  (d) If the judge denies the post-sentence motion, the judge promptly shall issue an order and the order shall be filed and served as provided in Rule 114.

  (e) If the defendant withdraws a post-sentence motion, the judge promptly shall issue an order memorializing the withdrawal, and the order shall be filed and served as provided in Rule 114.

- A motion challenging the validity of a plea of guilty or nolo contendere, or the denial of a motion to withdraw a plea of guilty or *nolo contendere*
- A motion for judgment of acquittal
- A motion in arrest of judgment
- A motion for a new trial
- A motion to modify the sentence

The Post-Sentence Memorandum serves as an opportunity for the trial judge to correct errors prior to appeal. Except in rare cases, the judge will issue a written decision on the errors raised in the Post-Sentence Memorandum. The judge has 120 days from the filing of the Post-Sentence Memorandum to issue a written decision. If the judge does not issue the decision within 120 days, the requests for relief in the memorandum will be considered denied by the operation of law.

Direct Appeal

You have 30 days from the issuance of the judge's decision on the Post-Sentencing Memorandum to file a notice of intent appeal. Failure to file a timely notice of appeal can result in the loss of your right to file an appeal. The notice is filed with the trial judge. The trial judge will then issue an order indicating that the defendant has 21 days to file a document informing the court of the errors that the defendant will raise on appeal. This is called a "Statement of Errors Complained of on Appeal," and is required by the Pennsylvania Rule of Appellate Procedure 1925. All appeals in criminal cases are handled by the Pennsylvania Superior Court. When the Superior Court receives notice of the appeal, and while the trial judge is writing a written response to the statement of errors, the Superior Court will issue a docketing statement to the Defendant's attorney requesting additional information regarding the case. This statement must be carefully completed and returned to the court.

After the trial court issues its opinion, the record of trial is transmitted to the Pennsylvania Superior Court. The court will order that the appellant (in criminal cases this is the defendant who files an appeal of their conviction or sentence) file their brief and a reproduced record[18] within approximately 40 days of the order. The brief in an appeal is the appellant's written arguments that explain why they are entitled to relief. The written brief is the most important part of an appeal and requires careful research and preparation.

---

[18] The reproduced record is a collection of the materials necessary for the appellate court to decide the case. Depending on what happened during the trial and what issues are raised on appeal, what is required to be included in the reproduced record will vary. What is important to note is that the appellate court will not consider matters that are not part of the record.

After the appellant's brief is filed, the appellee (the Commonwealth in criminal cases) has 30 days to file its brief. The Commonwealth's brief will focus on arguments that defend what happened at trial and sentencing and ask the court to deny relief. In response to the Commonwealth, the appellant may, if necessary, file a reply brief 14 days after service of the appellee's brief. The purpose of the reply brief is to respond to arguments in the appellee's brief.

After the submission of briefs, the Superior court will set a date for oral argument. During oral argument, the attorneys for each side will have the opportunity to state why they believe their position is correct. The judges will often interrupt the attorneys to ask specific questions during the oral argument.

After oral argument, the case is submitted for consideration by a three-judge panel of the Superior Court for a decision. After discussion, the judges vote, and the majority wins. Decisions may be made in a few days, but often it takes several months.

The party who loses an appeal in the Superior Court is permitted to request that a larger group of that Court's judges review the case. This request must be made in a motion arguing why the panel's decision was wrong. This is granted in rare cases and is called an *en banc* appeal. The procedure with the briefing process described above begins again.

The losing party is also able to ask the Pennsylvania Supreme Court to review the case. Such a request must be filed within 30 days of the Superior Court's most recent decision. There is no right to review before the Pennsylvania Supreme Court; therefore, a petition asking the Court to hear the case must be filed. If the Court agrees to accept the case for review, the party seeking appeal files its brief first. The winning party from the Superior Court then files a responsive brief; after that, the party seeking appeal may file a reply brief.

If a defendant loses their appeal before the Superior Court and the Pennsylvania Supreme Court denies their request to review the case, their direct appeal is final, and the judgment in their case is considered final.

Post-Conviction Relief

The final way to seek relief from a wrongful conviction or unjust sentence in Pennsylvania comes from the Post-Conviction Relief Act (PCRA).[19] Requests for relief pursuant to the PCRA must be filed within one year from the date an appeal is final or if more than one year has passed, within 60 days after the discovery of an error. These deadlines are

---

[19] 42 Pa.C.S.A. §9541 *et seq.*

considered jurisdictional, meaning that if you do not file within the deadline, the court does not have the legal authority to grant relief. The ability to obtain relief under the PRCA is generally limited to certain legal issues, but it is not impossible to obtain relief. I have assisted a client who was in prison for more than 20 years and obtained relief when we discovered an error in his case related to the prosecution's intentional suppression of evidence. In those cases, the defendant must show that they filed their request for relief within 60 days of the discovery of the error and that misconduct by the prosecution or a mistake (called ineffective assistance of counsel) by a defense attorney prevented them from discovering the error earlier.

Right to Counsel

It is the responsibility of the defense attorney that represented you at trial to represent you during the sentencing phase of your case and to file the post-sentence memorandum. Typically, you will either hire the attorney that represented you at trial or a new attorney to represent you on appeal. If you qualify financially you may request the court appoint a new attorney to represent you on appeal.

If you are convicted at trial, you have important post-trial and appellate rights. It is critical that you understand those rights and take advantage of every opportunity to obtain relief. Although relief on appeal is rare, it is not impossible, and anyone who has been wrongfully convicted or unjustly sentenced should not give up until they have exhausted every reasonable legal option to obtain relief.

Chapter 12

What Are the Most Common Offenses in Pennsylvania?

Every case and every defendant is unique. The discussion of so-called common offenses in this chapter is not designed to be all-encompassing but does provide important information regarding the crimes that make up the majority of criminal charges in Pennsylvania.

Driving Under the Influence (DUI)

Thousands of drivers are arrested every year in Pennsylvania for DUI. A conviction for DUI in Pennsylvania can have serious legal consequences. Even a first offense DUI conviction can be punished with a hefty fine, a driver's license suspension, and for some first-time offenders, a jail sentence. A DUI conviction can also have other consequences outside of the legal process and may affect your life negatively in the future. A DUI conviction can put your employment at risk and make it difficult to obtain any work that requires driving as part of your job responsibilities. A DUI conviction will considerably increase the cost of your automobile insurance. If you hold a professional license, a conviction may trigger disciplinary action by your professional licensing board, and if you are an immigrant, a DUI conviction may put you at risk for deportation.

A driver may face a DUI charge if they drive with a blood alcohol content (BAC) level at 0.08 percent or higher, even if that motorist's driving ability is not actually impaired. Similarly, if you appear impaired, you can be charged with DUI even with a BAC level below 0.08 percent.

The BAC measurement is a key factor when it comes to sentencing DUI offenders:

- "General" impairment means a BAC measurement ranging from 0.08 to 0.099 percent.
- A "high" BAC measurement ranges from 0.10 to 0.159 percent.
- The "highest" BAC measurement is 0.16 percent or higher.

- A driver under 21 years of age may be charged with driving under the influence if that driver's BAC level measures at 0.02 percent or higher.

In some DUI cases, the law requires at least a few days in jail. Mandatory minimum jail terms for Pennsylvania DUI convictions are:

- For the first offense with general impairment, jail time is not mandatory. Two days is the possible jail sentence for a first offense with a high BAC level, and three days is the possible jail sentence for the highest BAC level

- For a second offense with general impairment, five days of jail time is required. Thirty days is the jail sentence for a second offense with a high BAC level, and ninety days is the jail sentence for the highest BAC level

- For the third offense with general impairment, ten days of jail time is required. Ninety days is the jail sentence for a third offense with a high BAC level, and one year is the sentence for the highest BAC level

A DUI conviction may be charged as a felony when an intoxicated driver causes an injury or fatality. When that happens, that driver may face one of Pennsylvania's three felony DUI charges:

- Homicide While Under the Influence: This is a second-degree felony, the most severe DUI charge that a motorist may face in this state. A conviction may be penalized with a five-to-ten-year prison term and a fine of up to $25,000.

- Aggravated Assault While Under the Influence: This is also a second-degree felony charge that may be brought when an intoxicated motorist seriously or permanently injures someone.

- Felony DUI with Injury: Typically, this is the charge when an intoxicated motorist injures someone. A good DUI lawyer might be able to have the charge lowered to a misdemeanor DUI.

In addition to understanding the potential penalties, it is critical to understand the impact of a DUI conviction on your ability to drive. Below are the ignition interlock device (IID) and driver's license suspension rules for the general, highest, and highest impairment rates and for first, second, and subsequent driving under the influence offenses in Pennsylvania.

For general impairment:

- First offense: no license suspension
- Second offense: a 12-month license suspension with IID eligibility after 6 months. The IID must be used for a period of 1 year.
- Subsequent offenses: a 12-month license suspension with IID eligibility after 6 months. The IID must be used for a period of 1 year.

For high rate impairment:

- First offense: a 12-month license suspension with immediate IID eligibility. The IID must be used for a period of 1 year.
- Second offense: a 12-month license suspension with IID eligibility after 6 months. The IID must be used for a period of 1 year.
- Subsequent offenses: an 18-month license suspension with IID eligibility after 9 months. The IID must be used for a period of 1 year.

For highest rate impairment:

- First offense: a 12-month license suspension with immediate IID eligibility. The IID must be used for a period of 1 year.

- Second offense: an 18-month license suspension with IID eligibility after 9 months. The IID must be used for a period of 1 year.
- Subsequent offenses: an 18-month license suspension with IID eligibility after 9 months. The IID must be used for a period of 1 year.

To start a vehicle that is equipped with an ignition interlock device, a driver must blow into the IID, which is essentially a miniature breathalyzer device. If a driver's blood alcohol content level is detectable, the vehicle does not start. An IID is not cheap. They cost between $650 to $1,100 unless an offender qualifies for an exemption based on financial hardship. When a driver qualifies for that exemption, the state will pay part or all of the IID's cost.

Sex Crimes

More than 4,000 rapes were reported in Pennsylvania in 2018. Thousands of other sex crimes—both felonies and misdemeanors—are also reported each year. Rape and sexual assault are among the most heinous crimes prosecuted in the criminal justice system. The psychological and emotional damage to the victim of a serious sex crime lasts for a lifetime. Thus, the Pennsylvania criminal courts harshly punish those who are convicted of serious sex crimes, and no leniency can be expected.

That said, false allegations of rape or sexual assault can also destroy a person's life. Pennsylvania law ensures that the consequences of a sex crime conviction are long-lasting by requiring offenders to register with the state's sex offender database. Years of experience have taught me that sex crime accusations can be exaggerated or entirely fabricated by persons who—for whatever reason—are jealous, mistaken, or simply seeking revenge.

Sex crimes are part of a large category of crimes under Pennsylvania law, ranging from indecent exposure in public to forcible rape. Some sex crimes are misdemeanors, but others are felonies. The sex crimes that are considered serious felonies include:

- Rape and statutory rape
- Sexual assault and statutory sexual assault
- Institutional sexual assault
- Aggravated indecent assault
- Involuntary deviate sexual intercourse

Rape is a first-degree felony in Pennsylvania. Rape is defined by Pennsylvania statutes as sexual intercourse with another person in these circumstances:

- When force is used to compel the victim
- When a threat is made that prevents resistance by the victim
- When the victim is unconscious
- When the perpetrator knows that the victim is unaware of the perpetrator's actions
- When the perpetrator administers a drug or intoxicant without the victim's consent
- When the victim cannot legally consent because of a mental disability

A rape conviction in Pennsylvania is punishable with a prison term of up to twenty years and a fine of up to $25,000. Another ten years and a $100,000 fine may be imposed if the offender administered a substance that induced euphoria or memory loss to prevent resistance.

The rape of anyone below the age of 13 can be punished upon conviction with a prison term of up to forty years, and if a minor is seriously injured, a convicted offender may be sentenced to life in prison.

In addition to rape, several other sex crimes are considered serious felonies. These include "statutory" sexual assault and "institutional" sexual assault.

Statutory sexual assault is usually called statutory rape. It is sexual intercourse with a minor under age 16 if the perpetrator is at least four years older. The crime is a second-degree felony unless the age difference is eleven years or more; in that case, the charge is a first-degree felony.

Institutional sexual assault happens when a perpetrator has, according to Pennsylvania law, "sexual intercourse, deviate sexual intercourse, or indecent contact with an inmate, detainee, patient or resident."

To be charged with institutional sexual assault, the perpetrator must be a volunteer or employee of an institution and must know that the victim is an "inmate, detainee, patient, or resident." Institutions include but are not limited to:

- Hospitals and other medical treatment facilities
- Prisons, jails, and "halfway" house facilities
- Schools and churches
- Daycare facilities and sports organizations
- Summer camps, senior centers, and nursing homes

Involuntary deviate sexual intercourse is the charge when a victim is raped with an object or is otherwise forced, threatened, or made impaired in order to commit "unnatural" acts. Involuntary deviate sexual intercourse is a first-degree felony in Pennsylvania. The penalties for a first-degree felony conviction include ten to twenty years in prison and a fine of up to $25,000.

Indecent assault is a crime that happens when a perpetrator has "indecent" contact with a victim, causes the victim to have indecent contact with the perpetrator, or causes the victim to come into contact with semen, urine, or feces for the purpose of satisfying the perpetrator sexually. Indecent assault is committed by force or the threat of force, when a victim is unconscious or incapable of consent, when an assailant impairs a victim with drugs or alcohol when a victim is below 13 years old, or the victim is under 16, and the perpetrator is more than four years older. Depending upon the details of the case, indecent assault may be prosecuted as a misdemeanor or as a felony.

Drug Crimes

More than five thousand drug overdose deaths were reported in Pennsylvania in 2017. Drug abuse continues to be one of the most pressing legal and social problems in the United States. In 2018, more than 1.6 million people were arrested in this nation on various drug charges.

Often drug crimes in Pennsylvania involve the recreational use of marijuana. In 2016, medical marijuana became legal in Pennsylvania for a small number of medical conditions. Marijuana may be possessed and used only with a doctor's approval.

Marijuana use and possession remain illegal under federal law and for recreational or unauthorized medical use in Pennsylvania. In fact, in 2017, Pennsylvania law enforcement officers made more than 27,000 arrests for possession of marijuana. A first-offense conviction for possessing thirty grams or less of marijuana—"simple" possession—is a misdemeanor conviction in Pennsylvania, and the maximum penalty is a jail term of thirty days and a fine of $500.

Some Pennsylvania cities and municipalities, however, have adopted their own marijuana ordinances with lesser penalties. In Pittsburgh and Philadelphia, for example, it's a $25 fine if you are convicted for possessing thirty grams or less of marijuana. In Harrisburg, the fine is $75.

If someone in Pennsylvania possesses a small quantity of an illegal drug other than marijuana for their personal use, that person will usually be charged with a misdemeanor punishable by a $500 fine and up to a year in jail. However, the possession of PCP, LSD, cocaine, methamphetamine, medical isomers, or more than one thousand pounds of marijuana can be charged as a felony punishable upon conviction with a two-to-ten-year prison term and a fine of up to $2,500.

Possession "with intent to deliver" PCP, LSD, cocaine, methamphetamine, medical isomers, or more than one thousand pounds of marijuana is punishable upon conviction with up to twenty-five years in prison and a $250,000 fine (the fine may be higher if profits from the sale of illegal drugs surpassed $250,000).

Cultivating or manufacturing drugs illegally may be a felony or a misdemeanor. The charge will depend on the drug and the particular circumstances of the case. A felony charge for manufacturing or cultivating drugs illegally can be penalized upon conviction with a fifteen-year prison term.

It is also illegal—a first-degree misdemeanor—to possess drug paraphernalia in Pennsylvania. Drug paraphernalia is defined as any device, which is used or is intended to be used for the purpose of planting, propagating, cultivating, growing, harvesting, manufacturing, compounding, converting, producing, processing, preparing, testing, analyzing, packing, repacking, storing, containing, concealing, injecting, ingesting, inhaling or otherwise introducing into the human body a controlled substance in violation of the Drug Device and Cosmetic Act.[20] That is a very broad definition. Most of the time, drug paraphernalia charges result from the possession of things like bowls, bongs, rolling papers, needles, and razor blades. However, the definition is broad enough to include a plastic bag containing marijuana. Because of this broad definition,

---

[20] 35 Pa.C.S.A. § 780-113(a)(32).

it is common for individuals charged with drug possession to also be charged with possessing drug paraphernalia. The maximum penalty for a paraphernalia possession conviction is a year in jail and a $2,500 fine.

As with many other crimes, drug convictions may have significant collateral consequences. And any drug conviction—even for simple marijuana possession—may:

- Disqualify you for public benefits
- Disqualify you for federal financial aid
- Make it difficult to retain or find employment
- Make it difficult to find a residence to rent
- Make it difficult to obtain a professional license
- Make it more difficult to get accepted into a college or other education programs

Every Pennsylvania drug crime conviction is also penalized with a suspension of the offender's driver's license, even if no vehicle played any part in the crime. A first drug crime conviction triggers a six-month suspension. For a second conviction, the suspension period is one year.

Assault and Battery

Assault and battery are legal terms that are generally used to describe placing someone in fear of injury or actually causing injury by hitting or striking them, including the use of an object or weapon. Commonly an assault is defined as placing someone in fear of being hit or injured, while battery refers to actually hitting or striking someone. Unlike many states, Pennsylvania doesn't have a specific law that uses the term "battery." Instead, the state defines and forbids "simple assault" and "aggravated assault." Simple assault is usually charged as a misdemeanor, but there is nothing "simple" about the law or about what follows an arrest.

To convict someone of simple assault, a prosecutor must prove that a defendant recklessly or intentionally committed at least one of these acts:

- put someone in fear of imminent bodily injury,
- attempted to inflict bodily injury on someone else, or
- did in fact inflict bodily injury on another person.

In Pennsylvania, simple assault is usually a second-degree misdemeanor, but if the victim was younger than age 12 and the defendant is age 18 or older, the offense can be charged as a first-degree misdemeanor.

Aggravated assault in Pennsylvania is "the attempt to cause serious bodily harm to another," or if bodily injury occurs, and the defendant shows "extreme indifference to the value of human life." Aggravated or "felony" assault may be charged as a second or first-degree felony.

Every assault with a deadly weapon is considered an aggravated assault. And even if an injury or an attempt to cause injury was not "serious," aggravated assault can be charged if the alleged victim is a first responder, judge, teacher, police officer, corrections officer, or a child.

A conviction for aggravated assault as a second-degree felony may be penalized with up to ten years in prison and/or a fine of up to $25,000.

If an aggravated assault results in serious bodily injuries, or if a prosecutor alleges that a defendant specifically attempted to cause serious bodily injuries, the prosecutor may charge that defendant with first-degree felony aggravated assault. Aggravated assault charged as a first-degree felony is one of the most serious crimes dealt with by the Pennsylvania criminal justice system. A first-degree felony conviction for aggravated assault may be penalized with up to twenty years in prison and/or a fine of up to $25,000.

Domestic assault is not considered a separate crime in Pennsylvania, but if an alleged assault against a household or family member is reported, police are required to make an arrest, and a victim may not "drop" the charge—that decision is left entirely to the prosecutor.

Any assault conviction in Pennsylvania can dramatically and negatively change your life. In addition to criminal charges and penalties, assault in Pennsylvania is an "intentional tort," which means that victims may also sue their assailants for damages. An assault or aggravated assault conviction has consequences that can follow an offender for years. An assault conviction will appear on your criminal record, which means that it can be seen by anyone who conducts a background check.

If you hold a professional license in this state, an assault conviction will likely mean disciplinary action—a suspension or revocation of your license—by your professional licensing board. If you are an immigrant in Pennsylvania, an assault conviction may put you at risk for deportation.

Theft Crimes

In everyday conversation, most of us use the words "theft" and "robbery" interchangeably, but theft and robbery are actually different crimes in Pennsylvania.

Theft is any unauthorized taking of another person's property, but robbery is a specific type of theft accompanied by force or intimidation. In other words, legally speaking, all robberies are thefts, but not all thefts are robberies.

To convict someone of theft, a prosecutor must prove beyond a reasonable doubt that a defendant unlawfully took property that legally belonged to someone else with the intention of depriving the rightful owner of that property. You can also be convicted of a theft charge if you accept or receive stolen property, when you know it is stolen, and you do not intend to return it to its rightful owner.

The penalty for a theft conviction depends on the value of the stolen property. Listed here is a brief summary of Pennsylvania's theft laws and the penalties for theft convictions:

- When stolen property is valued at or below $50, theft is a third-degree misdemeanor punishable upon conviction with up to a year in jail and/or a fine of up to $2,500

- When stolen property is valued at more than $50 but at or below $200, theft is a second-degree misdemeanor punishable upon conviction with up to two years in prison and/or a fine of up to $5,000

- When stolen property is valued at more than $200 but at or below $2,000, theft is a first-degree misdemeanor punishable upon conviction with up to five years in prison and/or a fine of up to $10,000

- When stolen property is valued at or above $2,000, theft is a third-degree felony punishable upon conviction with up to seven years in prison and/or a fine of up to $15,000. The theft of any motorized vehicle in Pennsylvania is also a third-degree felony

- If a firearm is stolen or if theft is committed in a designated disaster situation, theft is a second-degree felony punishable upon conviction with up to ten years in prison and/or a fine of up to $25,000

- If you receive stolen property and that stolen property is a firearm, the charge is a first-degree felony punishable upon conviction with up to twenty years in prison and/or a fine of up to $25,000

The penalty for any theft conviction can be "enhanced"—that is, harsher—if a firearm was used, if a minor was involved, or if the defendant has previous criminal convictions.

In addition to legal penalties, theft convictions have significant collateral consequences. A theft conviction goes on your criminal record, so it can be seen by anyone who is conducting a background check. If you hold a professional license in Pennsylvania, a theft conviction is apt to trigger disciplinary action—the suspension or revocation of your license—by your professional licensing board. If you're an immigrant, a conviction for theft could put you at risk for deportation.

Chapter 13

What Is the Best Way to Defend My Case?

There is, of course, no silver bullet or secret tactic that defendants or their defense team can employ to ensure they achieve the best possible outcome. Any attorney that believes that there is, guarantees victory, or claims to have never lost a case is either dishonest or has simply not tried any difficult cases. Despite this reality, anyone facing criminal charges can and should learn as much as they can about the law, their case, and be an active participant in their defense. I always recommend that clients and their family keep some of the following tips in mind as they prepare for trial.

Pick the Right Team

It is critical that you have the right defense team to represent you at all stages of the process. The advantage of court-appointed counsel is that they represent defendants who qualify free of charge. There are many public defenders that are competent, dedicated, and sincerely do everything they can to fight for their clients. But there are limitations. Many public defenders are overworked and underpaid. Often, they are in their initial job after law school and are forced by the system to engage in legal triage. With rare exceptions they will not be appointed until after an investigation is complete and a defendant has been charged. This means that critical rights may have been waived and opportunities to obtain evidence have been lost. It is for these reasons that many defendants who would qualify for a public defender will rely on friends and family for assistance to hire an attorney to represent them.

Once the decision is made to invest in an attorney, the attorney you hire should have the right experience, inside and importantly outside the courtroom. There are many attorneys that will represent anyone facing any type of criminal charge even though they have only practiced law for a few years and do not have significant experience in jury trials. Understand, while basic litigation skills are important in any courtroom, it is crucial that your defense team is led by an experienced attorney who knows how to fight and win in the courtroom and also understands how to speak credibly to a jury. The questions outlined in the "Know Your Rights" chapter of this book, specifically questions about experience and philosophy of trial preparation, are critical for ensuring you hire the right attorney for your case.

With regard to experience, a defendant should know if their attorney has successfully tried cases involving the specific charges they face and similar factual circumstances, and they should know if their attorney has spent enough time in the courtroom trying litigated cases that they truly understand how the juries think and make decisions.

Questions related to trial preparation and philosophy should involve asking about the expert witnesses and investigators an attorney has worked with in the past as well as how they plan to involve the client in the development of the case. You should never be afraid to ask an attorney about the time and attention they have to put into your case. Criminal defense should not be treated as a commodity because your life and future are at stake.

The best attorneys are those who dedicate themselves fully to a limited number of cases so that they can ensure they are fully prepared and focused on each individual case. The explanations here and the sample questions in the

"Know Your Rights" chapter can be applied to court-appointed counsel and any attorney you consider hiring.

When you are in a fight for your future and freedom, it is critical you have an attorney you feel comfortable communicating with, who understands your case, and who has the passion and skills to zealously and effectively represent you.

Ask Questions and Be Proactive

Defendants and their families must not be afraid to ask questions about their case, the defense strategy, and the process. Most people would not choose a doctor for a risky surgery without asking questions and making sure they understand the skill and experience of the surgeon and the procedure they will use. Criminal cases are life-altering events, and it is critical that any defendant facing trial does everything they can to ask the right questions and remain engaged and involved in their defense. One of the best things defendants can do is ask their defense team repeatedly and often, "what can I do to help" or "what do you need from me."

Listen to the Right Advice

After you have picked your team, asked the right questions, and done everything you can to educate yourself on the process, you need to be prepared to listen to the advice you are given by your attorneys and the people in your life that you trust.

Aside from your attorney and your most trusted friends or family, you should be very careful not to rely on bad advice. The world is full of "Jailhouse Lawyers" (know-it-all types with no legal training, experience, or expertise) who will gladly share their ideas or opinions about a case or how it should be defended. Although many might mean well, in my experience, it is extremely dangerous to rely on the guidance of anyone that is eagerly offering advice in this manner. Jails and society at large remain full of rumors and misunderstandings about the law. In fact, even if a Jailhouse Lawyer had some past experience, the rapid changes in the law make many of the supposed lessons learned from those old "war stories" irrelevant to the current law. Even worse is when law enforcement pretends to befriend someone who is under investigation and offers them guidance. Remember, there is no confidentiality or attorney-client privilege with anyone other than your defense attorney. Anyone else can potentially be turned into a witness against you.

Ultimately, when you are charged it is the Commonwealth versus you. No one, especially not law enforcement is on your side other than your legal defense team.

Chapter 14

What Can I Do Now to Prepare for Trial?

The goal of the final chapter of this book is to provide those facing charges with a few final ideas that may prove useful in the preparation of their case. These are ideas I began thinking about when I was a prosecutor and continue to use in my practice today. With rare exceptions, I request the following information from my clients in every case.

Although attorneys may request different or additional information, I highly recommend that you gather this type of information as early as possible in your case.

Stop Talking about Your Case

Do not talk to anyone about the specifics of your case unless they are part of your defense team, and your attorney is comfortable with the release of information. Anyone other than an attorney could be subpoenaed and turned into a witness against you. This includes email and social media. Anything you write or post can be used against you. Prosecutors will be reviewing your social media posts and can in some cases, attempt to subpoena your email and bank records.

Interrogation Memory Dump

If you waive your right to remain silent and choose to submit to questioning by law enforcement, you should draft a document for your attorney that provides as much detail as you can remember about the interrogation. This includes a discussion of what occurred during the interview and anything you can remember about the questions you were asked. You should always include a description of what happened, how long each stage of the interview process took, and what was said if/when you were read your *Miranda* rights.

Search and Seizure Questionnaire

You should take notes and provide as much detail as possible regarding anything that law enforcement took from you during the investigation. This includes DNA samples, blood samples, urine samples, clothes, cell phones, computers, and anything else. It is critical that defense attorneys know what was taken and how it was obtained. Specifically, was a search warrant issued, or did you consent? This information can be critical in taking steps during the investigation to revoke any consent you may have given for a search and to ensure that your Fourth Amendment rights are protected.

List of Potential Fact and Character Witnesses

A critical part of preparing for trial will involve the independent investigation of defense counsel. You should not contact potential witnesses yourself, but you should create a detailed list for your attorney that includes the name, email address, phone, and basic information about each witness. You should explain how they know the witness and why you believe the witness may have helpful information for the case. This list should include not only people that may have witnessed some aspect of the events leading to the charges; it should include people who know you well and may be able to testify regarding your character at trial.

Review the Report of Investigation

Law enforcement will produce a document that is a report of their investigation. This document will include summaries of witness interviews, investigative actions, pictures, evidence, and copies of witness statements. I always ask my clients to review that report thoroughly, take detailed notes and provide them to me. You should be engaged in this process with your attorney and make sure that you are intimately familiar with the evidence the government has in your case. This should include reviewing the recordings of interviews that were made as part of the investigation.

Remember this is your case. You and your attorneys should be working as a team and your insight and thoughts on the investigation matter.

Biography

It is critical that an attorney understands who their client is, where they come from, and what is most important to them. In your own words, you should draft a life history that explains every significant event and helps your defense team understand where you come from and who you are. This biography should answer the basic questions of where you are from, where you grew up, what your family life and childhood were like (good and bad).

Stay Positive

The criminal justice process can be intimidating and frustrating. There will be highs and lows. While no one can control the final outcome of their case, the system, while flawed, is based on principles that are designed to protect the innocent. Ultimately, the most important decision of your life will be made by a jury of your peers, and as Thomas Jefferson wrote, "I consider trial by jury as the only anchor ever yet imagined by man, by which a government can be held to the principles of its constitution." As long as we have jury trials and a healthy respect for the constitution, there is hope that the average citizen can and will receive a fair trial.

About the Author

Attorney R. Davis Younts is the founder and owner of R. Davis Younts, Esquire, LLC. He represents military clients worldwide and provides criminal defense services in state and federal court in his home state of Pennsylvania. He is a 1999 graduate of Liberty University, and he earned his Juris Doctor in 2002 from the Dickinson School of Law of the Pennsylvania State University and a Masters of Military Operational Arts and Sciences from Air University in 2012. He has been recognized for his trial advocacy skills by induction into the Order of the Barristers, receipt of Air Force Judge Advocate General's School Association of Trial Lawyers of America Trial Advocacy Award, and was rated as the number one Senior Defense Counsel in the Air Force in 2011.

In September of 2001, he was a law student at the Dickinson School of Law in Carlisle, Pennsylvania. On September 11th, he was on his way to a class on Tax Law when he heard the news that planes flown by terrorists had hit both towers of the World Trade Center. The events of that unforgettable day prompted him to dedicate his legal studies and career to defend the freedom of all Americans. After graduating from law school, he became an officer in the United States Air Force. As an active duty JAG, he served as a prosecutor, a defense attorney, a command legal advisor, and a senior legal advisor to deployed commanders and general officers. He also served as the Chief of the Military Justice Division at the Air Force JAG School and served as an editor of past editions of the book *The Military Commander and the Law*. He continues his military service as a Lieutenant Colonel in the Air Force Reserves.

26 N 9th St, Lemoyne, PA 17043
(833) 739-5291 & (717) 340-4980
davis@yountslaw.com

9 781734 849448